AT THE TAWANG MONASTERY

Tapati Baruah Kashyap

First published in 2021 by
Becomeshakespeare.com

One Point Six Technologies Pvt Ltd.119-123, 1st Floor, Building J2, B - Wing, WadalaTruck Terminal, Wadala East, Mumbai, Maharashtra, India, 400022.T:+91 8080226699

© ISBN - 978-93-5458-124-3

To Maa,

Pursuing your creative spirit,

I would like to visit Tawang again.

Would you come with me?

CONTENTS

1	At the Rumtek Monastery	7
2	Namsai	9
3	At Buddha's feet	11
4	Meeting Chau Khouk Manpoong	12
5	Digging wisdom at Nalanda	14
6.	Loitering around Rajgir	18
7.	Makhdum Kund	20
8.	Venuvan	21
9.	At the slanting corner	22
10.	The layers of the mountain	24
11.	Sunset at Kaliabhomora	25
12.	Four elephants	27
13.	With Monpa ladies..	28
14.	At Dirang Valley	30
15.	Listening to Nature	32
16.	The forlorn guest house	33
17.	Welcome Sela	35
18.	The elderly monk	37
19.	The Himalayan echo	39
20.	The temple	40
21.	Sacred music	42
22.	Unseen beauty	44
23.	A memorable pilgrimage	45

24. The Battle of Nyokmadong   46

25. War on Buddha   48

26. The Sessa Durga Temple   50

27. The height with warmth   51

28. Nechiphu   52

29. Bomdila   53

30. Jaswant : A tribute   54

31. Into Suryapahar   55

32. The land, the people   57

33. A Land of happiness   59

34. Karma   60

35. Four noble truths   61

36. The monks at Ugyenling   62

37. A storehouse of wisdom   63

38. In search of Bhutan   64

39. Lady with a smile   66

40. A prayer at Dochula   67

41. Rebeka   68

42. A poem for Thimphu   70

43. National Memorial Chorten   71

44. The silent guest house   72

45. At the Tawang Monastery   73

46. The Museum   76

47. Remembering Rupa   78

48. Ani Gompa   80

49. Standing at Bumla   81

AT THE RUMTEK MONASTERY

The intensity of cold at the steps of the entrance,

prepared ourselves

for our pure prayer.....

firm and untainted, like the green trees beside.

Exactly, after twenty years,

I keep recalling

that unique moment....

of those memories, still lively

like a flowing river..

my inner being

pure and peaceful...

sublime too with blessings

of Lord Buddha.

Occasioned to revisit

by the mild first shower of

the new year..

though visited the monastery several years ago.

Yet I continue reminiscing

the divine presence of Lord Buddha.

My very first visit to a monastery,

where I discovered sanctity with faith,

as I offered prayer

in that Himalayan heaven,

up, in Sikkim,

I was bound to be happy and cheerful,

like the far-flung sky above,

the expanse of green below..

NAMSAI

"Namsai!

You will remain in my heart forever!"

I told myself.

Treading the footsteps of my father,

I was there at the forest guest house,

when the morning sun, with promises distinct,

more transparent than the water

of the Lohit flowing by,

and the chilly breeze

blowing from the Noa-Dihing

welcomed me.

As I stepped into the small town,

the wind from the distant ridges

of the snowclad eastern Himalayas,

kept touching every corner of my sleepy heart.

There were monks all over,

In red, yellow and saffron,

chanting hymns, silently

as the wiser ones with

their erudite discourse ,

showered enough strength

to console everyone's fiery souls.

Rightfully relevant to every heart

who were on the path of enlightenment?

and the moment seemed to be

the finest way of spending one's restless time.

Listening to Venerable Dr Dhammapiya's speech

how everyone is capable of becoming wise and,

Venerable Bhikkhu Panyaloka's sublime speech

spontaneously sprang from the core of their hearts…

I saw the little and the elderly monks

listening to the pearls of wisdom

with same patience.

I, as a novice, derived inspiration alike.

AT BUDDHA'S FEET

I looked up...

So huge, so divine..

Is it an ovation offered by

God's progeny?

At Dhamma Hill,where huge trees with green shadows

Stand upright and sing the song of humanity in unison.

I was awestruck to see God's grace

upon His children...

His creation..

Standing in the premises of the serene ground

I felt

how tiny and insignificant we all are...

on this planet called earth.

far away from Him

yet not far away from

the sweet sound of the flowing Lohit

blended with placid air, so did my spirit..

Standing at the feet of the colossal creation,

I felt like perceiving the four noble truths

Buddha inscribes.

MEETING CHAU KHOUK MANPOONG

Amidst the sprawling green campus,

the wooden house stands

like an epitome of peace,

befriending fresh air and silence around.

We went there to meet

a man

wise and erudite,

solely engaged to

revive his dearest mother-tongue, Tai-Khamti

welcoming us with sweet tea and biscuits.

Permitted were we to have a glimpse of

his study table inside...

he showed us a precious idol of Buddha,

His Holiness the Dalai Lama

had gifted him,

while leaving his country.

We were occasioned to reminisce

an episode of 1958.

We sat spellbound.

As we bade goodbye

he gifted us with a determined hand,

his three story books

written in Tai-Khamti, his dearest language,

in his windy, peaceful, sparkling

abode at Manmow, a tiny village...

In Namsai...

DIGGING WISDOM AT NALANDA

(i)

From Sikkim to Namsai

to Nalanda,

geographically a very long journey,

while for me,

a continuous journey it was

from one corner of the soul

to another.

(ii)

We began our pilgrimage,

visiting Hiuen Tsang's

museum at Nalanda's soil, where he had spent five long years.

We bowed down

to see his Godly presence

the air, the wide lake

bearing his memory

in wild.

The sun was

hot and healthy,

like the spark of my soul-searching spirit..

and to show us the shining past

of Nalanda!

A few water birds,

in the distant lake

either meditating upon

their prey

or to take rest,

we were not sure...

but we could comprehend..

the moment...

so divine and so pure,

no words at all

to define...

(iii)

The key rings,

booklets, earrings,

mementoes, replicas

of Lord Buddha....

small, big, glowing, attractive

enough to draw immediately

pilgrims like us...

I bought a few items

Recalling those faces of

my near and dear ones, back home.

(iv)
Showing the pass,
I entered the gate...
and had the real Nalanda
in front of my eyes.
The ruins of
the wise civilisation
and the endeavour to
dig out the wisdom....
lying underneath intact.

(v)
So many people around the world
gathered there to pick up
pearls of waning wisdom...
We talked to pilgrims from
Indonesia, Japan, Thailand and many other places.
All were passionate
to discover a past
overlapped with time and tide.
As we stepped into Nagarujana's bhavan,
we could perceive another dimension, another time..
with so much to know,
so much to read.
But our curiosity came to an end,
on the very last day of the Buddha Mahotsava,

as one monk went on narrating Vipassana,

the path to learning, peace and self discovery.

LOITERING AROUND RAJGIR

(i)

Loitering around that small

town of Rajgir, where roads were smooth

like the green foliage and the innocent hearts of the locals,

whose minds also seemed to be untainted,

for being far from the worldly comfort.

The tall and healthy trees inspired us to discover more.

Suddenly, we tended to feel,

we were so far,

even away from worldly duties and responsibilities.....

forgetting everything.....

amidst Nature and the vast sprawling campus....

But, at the end of the day, after an arduous attempt

to climb up the hill

in search of Shanti Stupa

for 20 minutes at a stretch...

we stopped midway and sat down on a piece of rock

gasping audibly...

unable to gather strength...

We came back with a weary heart

and eager to take much-needed rest.

Back in the guest house, I felt,

I must read and reread

the soul invigorating works

on Buddha,

so that I could climb,

up the Shanti Stupa, when I come here again.

(ii)

It was indeed an honest attempt to do the rightful.

Looking back to that precious moment

after exactly one year back...

I felt extremely reflective..

The old and sweet memories

filled my mind

with bliss and pleasure alike.

'Buddhodaya' -- a teacher's attempt to glorify Buddha,

'In search of Buddha in one night' and 'The Buddha in poet's vision'

with poetic sensibilities....

All those books dwindling

in my mind's eye like my own one...

MAKHDUM KUND

I had

very few words

to describe,

the hidden beauty of the place,

as I went on

discovering the conglomeration of faith

replete in Makhdum Kund

Shantidham and Vaitaranighat

around the place itself!

The twinkling sound of the tongas,

carrying people from one village to another,

the library of Sankar Jaiprasad, an eminent poet,

near Siddharth...

my tribute to that great poet and litterateur

came out naturally with reverence.

We visited the library...

searching the great poet amidst his huge collection of Hindi
books...

certainly, we did discover a heaven

on this earth!

VENUVAN

As we set out for a morning stroll,

the beautiful birds had already started

chirping from the branches of the trees around...

We met fresh wind,

with each stride...

....

Venuvan,

that Lord Buddha, had chosen

for divine meditation!

A place,

where one could meditate

for divine inspiration

infinitely?

The pond was then looking for another Buddha

at the same time engaged in attracting people profusely

like us

to its serene surrounding,

and also offered spaces to descend to

infinite meditation.

AT THE SLANTING CORNER

I was with Maya,

at this slanting corner of the hill.

She was entrusted with her obligation

to guide me.

So, was busy with showing me the memorable places,

for being a new comer to this place.

The living Buddha tradition attracts

anyone who could visit the land,

and people can follow the messages of

all Buddhist people here,

as one great pundit once told,

Buddhism itself is secular,

as one can follow the teachings

without being a Buddhist.

As it is the way of life....

I offered prayer at the sanctum sanctorum.

All was cleanly kept and well-ordered,

where erudite preachers

seen continuing the process of preaching.

I moved to feel the true colour

of the prevalent silence

wise and beautiful

with lots of food.

Maya, the Adi damsel,

who could speak fluent Assamese

told about the bike-riding disobedient youths,

consuming almost all the narcotics

available anywhere

behind those pan-shops.

Would those wise monks come out to

tell those youths--

"Shun your bad habits,

this is not the way

to meet God."

THE LAYERS OF THE MOUNTAIN...

I was not weary of visiting

this part of the globe,

Arunachal,

a place more for

the peace of mind,

a very dear place

with God's touches,

ubiquitously....

a real manifestation

of God's creative works…

Lost myself,

amidst the layers of the mountain..

I felt blessed

to move ahead

more such pleasures to unfold

more such beauties to behold...

SUNSET AT KOLIABHOMORA

It was a distinctive hour of the sunset,

while approaching the Koliabhomora…

the evening,

appeared to be exquisite.

The burning sun was swimming on the river,

and was about to rest in the bed of the horizon.

Our naked eyes could catch the sight in its reality,

a moment with divine grace,

we did not have words to define!

only we felt its benign presence

perhaps a very few of us

might have experienced such divine moment,

I attempted to catch the moment

with my limited strength,

my pen and petite pad...

I prayed to God,

'grant me strength to a great degree,

to express the unexpressed,

to enjoy with same strength

the sunrise and

the light after darkness'.

FOUR ELEPHANTS

Four elephants

greeted us during our Himalayan retreat

It was indeed a journey

to a great place with a great purpose.

That was our sixth visit to Lord Buddha's abode.

after visiting Chowkham, Namsai,

Nalanda, Bhutan, Suryapahar..

Now it was our pilgrimage to Tawang...

The blessings of

the elephant were absolute and fulfilling.

We were encouraged to proceed further.

We started late,

so the evening hours

raised our curiosity alarmingly..

amidst the whispering darkness of Nameri National Park...

we peeped from our car's window ..

fear and excitement at the back of our mind,

sticking to prayer consistently to cross the road safely

till we reached Tippi village.

WITH MONPA LADIES..

After climbing a few kilometres up

on the splendid Himalayas,

we saw a roadside tea stall,

to stop for inhaling fresh air

and also to have

a refreshing cup of tea....

The lady with a fresh smile

served us cups of steaming tea.

We exchanged a few warm words.

Her name was Umari,

A Monpa lady.

Her house was behind the small tea stall

where her ageing mother sitting

in the front yard and

basking in the little precious hilly sunshine,

they had then.

Loitering around her small hut,

we spotted skins of wild cats and dogs

dried up on the roof of their hut,

and a stack of straw and a bundle of fire-wood

lying in the veranda..

Refreshing ourselves thoroughly...

we bid

goodbye

to her smiling face

and also to

the beautiful place forever.

As we were nearing Dirang Valley,

we then stopped again,

to talk to Tezentima, Ringtin, Sanam, Tengzam and Pema,

toiling hard to build the mountain road,

to make both ends meet.

AT DIRANG VALLEY

We were then at NH 13,

the speed of our car,

lessened.

We had noticed,

the road side graffiti,

'Someone is waiting for you,

Drive slow'

Suddenly we were in front of

the beautiful Kameng river

rushing down to the plains with soothing sound...

Keeping prayers to God intact,

we drove through meandering paths with prayer flags

fluttering amid the tree..

and crossed

the Dirang Chhu.

The beautiful silent river,

welcomed us to Dirang valley,

surrounded by the layers of green mountain,

and tiny villages

perched on the hill-top.

We became curious

to see the other fold of the mountain...

LISTENING TO NATURE

A marvellous morning,

beside the dark mountain,

showering green messages

to our mind and spirit..

A green freshness...

blended with pristine purity

of souls of the surrounding mountain ...

We were lost in a chorus of

the wind, sun-light and the chirping birds around...

and the gliding river below...

We were in search of Tawang!

THE FORLORN GUEST HOUSE

The warm reception of a young couple

made our journey more comfortable,

as we were heading for

the lonely guest house

under the azure sky.

The dancing rivulet

showed us the way to the guest house gate.

And we headed

to spend the night

with the green forest

dotted with huge trees....

surrounded by cold silent darkness.

The dinner with boiled eggs, boiled leafy vegetables,

Bahadur Subba cooked in the lonely remote kitchen,

where wild animals used to roam profusely.

It was really nice to digest the invigorating cold...

with hot rice, salt and boiled fresh green vegetables,

the market was far away...

from that lonely guest house...

So Bahadur Subba had nothing much to offer

beside the dark green forest of the mountain.

We got up amidst freshness

around the silent folds of the Himalayas...

only to discover,

a fresh morning in a new place,

with so much of

Nature's warmth of paintings..

WELCOME SELA

(MON TAWANG Sela Pass)
(You are at an altitude of 13700 feet.
Welcome to Tawang)

As we reached the gate,
of Sela Pass
we discovered .....
chill in the air and the layers of the mountain wearing
the garlands of
floating flakes of snow…
even around us...
I could not imagine,
even I could not define
the intensity of cold
in Sela Pass...
We were being enveloped
by profound cold deeply...
only to get transported
to the divine world of cold and heavy wind...

My impulse

made me grope for words

for narrating the intensity of cold in

Sela Pass..

But undefined cold

accompanied by snow-flakes and wind

enlivened us thoroughly...

THE ELDERLY MONK

We met Gombu, the elderly monk in that cold afternoon.

He kept talking endlessly with the people who flowed in,

He seemed to be one with the age-old monastery.

For the last 76 years,

spending his time

atop the Eastern Himalayas!

The fresh smile in his face

encouraged everyone with an opportunity

to peep through,

the past of the Monastery

and his own past as well.

Even in that freezing cold,

his smile made his hue intact.

Next moment he led us

to the museum of the monastery.

Sitting in that sacred place,

decade after decade

he became like Lord Buddha,

a repository of wisdom

with each passing day.
I was convinced
of what Buddha said --
'Buddhism promotes
deeds that can beautify human mind.'

THE HIMALAYAN ECHO

Heading towards the dizzy heights

of the most revered mountain....

the birth place of Lord Shiva,

we tended to remain bereft of words....

No words on earth would match for

the picture.

Beauty-filled moment...

We were about 10,000 feet above sea-level!

Our hearts were not without humane touch..

to see those soldiers,

guarding our country dutifully

amidst the freezing cold...

We were not unaware of our fellow beings and relatives...

those who had failed to visit that transcendence...

those who had failed to grasp the encompassing beauty....

THE TEMPLE

Suddenly, we discovered the valley with a hilly rivulet beside.

Going ahead, we saw the signboard,

'Nag Mandir of 1966'.

Our car stopped and we climbed up

several steps to offer our

sincere prayers

to reach our destination safely.

………

Being atop the hill,

we saw the temple,

of Lord Shiva, the auspicious one,

and the soul of the universe

at that remote corner of the Himalayas.

We looked down below

as a mountain damsel turns into a little river

to jump along a rocky path

flowing joyfully and washing the feet of Lord Shiva.

We also heard her hilly songs,

resonating with the breeze,

blowing from beyond the mountain....
We could not find her name.
No one was there to tell us
about her....

SACRED MUSIC

The dark surrounding

of the guest house

made us

unsure about the music.

Yes, we were in a new place,

so curious to define

every new object.

What was just going on there?

We only heard a touching music,

The slashing wind....

The undefined music..

peeping out through the dark window,

we found only the whistling,

and gusty wind....

The day break

opened our eyes

fresh and wide.

We went out to find

the secret source of the music

of Tippi village....

It was the natural flow

of the glistening river

beside the guest house.

The flow with sweet sound

at the feet of the huge green mountain..

easily gripped our attention.

Listening to that sacred music,

overwhelmed we became.

The flow was fast,

but beautiful like a damsel

with no promise to stop

and look back.

But, we were about

to transcend....

unlike the descending Kameng

to our destined place, up..

UNSEEN BEAUTY

'The blacknecked cranes of Sangti

The guests from Siberia and China come to rest here...'

We expected to see them in abundance

without being to China.

We could learn from the local people,

even Bahadur Subba claimed with pride

how the surpassing beauty, the flock of

cranes carry to that corner

of the universe..

We could imagine only the marvellous beauty

of the divine creatures

along with the message of

the distant land.

But we could not stop for them,

yet the prospects of seeing them in near future

enlightened our journey

with curiosity more than ever.

A MEMORABLE PILGRIMAGE

We stopped to visit another sacred place,

on the road to Tawang..

The irresistible silence

unfolded before us,

a revered and a weighty

sacrific of the brave soldiers in the war,

fought in the chilly winter of nineteen sixty two.

Pondered over that unique phase of history

once again!

Are all those memories mere rocks of the past?

No, certainly not!

an honest attempt to preserve

their entire belongings

for the rest of the world

at that sacred place.

We offered our silent prayers

for those noble souls!

The nameless flowers around

shook their heads

perhaps to console our weeping hearts.

THE BATTLE OF NYOKMADONG

Stepping into the silent graveyard,

we were being swept by the wind

that resumed telling us a hidden chapter,

of nineteen sixty-two.

The silence here

replete with

heart touching history.

Young bravehearts from far-away villages

sleeping silently,

after a huge sacrifice..

at this lofty heights,

near Tawang.

Though cooled down the core of our spirit,

yet, it ignited our burning passion

to know more…

....

It was a supreme sacrifice to save the country

from the cruel clutches,

of our neighbour.

We bowed down

with a feeling of guilt

for our incapability to save them...

But, perhaps,

God above,

granted them

the blessings....

We stopped

and shed silent tears....

for their precious sacrifice....

A moment,

celestial and of utmost significance!

We too were indeed blessed!

WAR ON BUDDHA

The person was waiting for us.

Everyone knew him well.

His smiling face was enough to feel his inner self!

The distance lessened...

His wife with a cheerful face,

welcomed us...

with tasty fruits fresh from her garden.

Not to forget those taste,

we had borrowed some of them eagerly!

We began in English,

and did not realise when we shifted to Assamese

discovering their love for

the Assamese language.

'Your language is mine,' said they and

reciting a nursery rhyme,

taught by a teacher from the valley,

sixty years ago.

They used to study in Assamese medium school

once they were part of Assam.

A boundary gives one a new identity,

but nothing could mar

the innate passion .....

We were in search of "War on Buddha", a book he wrote.

The price is invaluable!

A book of his memories of a war,

that changed our lives..

spontaneously narrating in detail,

when he with his parents and whole villagers

running through the mountains, as the cannons roared,

and to escape from the cluthces of the enemy troops,

leaving behind their home and hearth.

THE SESSA DURGA TEMPLE

We stopped near the temple,

with a view to offer our obeisance.

Durga, the symbol of energy,

helps one regain one's strength

and vigour..

Our journey, now though ascending forward,

yet we were accompanied by our strength,

as we prayed recalling Her one hundred and eight names,

with specific supremacy...

We were blessed by the unseen power...

The smooth roads,

comforted us enough to proceed farther,

and to enjoy the charming beauties delightfully....

THE HEIGHT WITH WARMTH...

The height of the mountain,

opened new vistas for us…

to move ahead...

We were being transported

from mundane

to sublime.

Our mind certainly moved ahead of us....

The picture of my mother, getting up early,

for the sake of fulfilling her creative urge,

came to my mind immediately.

Reaching such heights,

I kept cherishing many such golden moments of life,

with regrets for many deeds yet to complete…

But the height brought to my mind,

the warmth of the past too,

with no distraction at all.

NECHIPHU...

The Eaglenest Wildlife Sanctury was sleeping silently...

And our journey accompanied

By the sparkling resonance of the Kameng,

suddenly got disconnected....

We were at a considerable height...

We were at Nechiphu...

we felt our ears blocked,

and we started transcending.....

'prepare for a long ascent,

with this height ahead,

this is just the beginning,'

the mountain whispered.

BOMDILA

We were nearing Bomdila.

Suddenly, the intensity of

cold increased.

It was more biting and wild,

we started shivering.

And had entered

a restaurant

called Siphiyang Phong,

to have steaming tea and also our lunch,

at that chilly afternoon.

Also realised

"This is the sign of approaching to Tawang,

our dream journey in reality."

A quick trip up nearby

and we visited Gontse Gaden Rabgyel Lling Monastery

to pray amidst cold,

with innate purity,

"I take refuge in you, O' Lord."

Buddham Saranam Gacchami.

JASWANT :A TRIBUTE

"Blow gently you winds, blow gently

Blow gently over this hallowed land

This is the place where Jaswant fought

the scene of his final stand."

A new poem

emerged in me,

as I merged my being in deep thought

into the eternal lines of

the poem,

written to glorify

the soul of Jaswant....

Our folded hands

prayed for the unseen..

The bright beautiful flowers

blooming beside beckoned us

to feel the bodiless presence...

of Jaswant..

in this remote corner of the Himalayas…

where green and silence coexist.

INTO SURYAPAHAR

The person came

near us…

as we bowed down

at the sanctum sanctorum,

of the Shiva-Vishnu temple.

All of a sudden,

started narrating,

the stories behind....

We moved from one cave to another..

Each one unfolded before us newer truth...

The engraved pictures of Lord Vishnu,

Shiva, Buddha, Mahavira and all

the godly birds and beasts,

signifying the divine hidden meaning,

of the supreme!

We were on the verge of realising

the confluence of faiths...

as we took the help of motor ride

to pay visit to the other corners of the

wide campus.....

When did Gautam Buddha

step into this corner

to meditate at this hill of the sun?

The well kept museum

unfolded before us more such exciting objects

of the distant past...

Is it history or is it a recovered past?

THE LAND, THE PEOPLE...

As the Monpa lady went on

relating her faith,

we were mere mute listeners then.

'We are the best architect...

and so also the Sherdukpens,

of the Kameng ..

with full faith in Buddhism..

we do believe that

Padmasambhava, the Indian monk from Nalanda,

who helped the Tibetans

establish Buddhism in the eighteenth century..'

They as descendants follow that virtuous path of peace...

Pleased to discover the simplicity

inherent in them,

we bade goodbye with

the memory of witnessing the sleeping Buddha

in profound peace!

The benign image came

to my mind…

again and again,

as we began climbing up,

in search of the divine truth.

A LAND OF HAPPINESS

Is that a cold and silent city?

No, it is

a land of happiness,

where people are bound to be happy

with limited and basic material gains.

Ignoring happiness

of the world around,

they are looking for...

when happiness is a way,

in this blissfully calm place.

Happiness is a self-constructed path..

the person standing next to us

kept talking to us…

'When three ridges come together, indeed, not a good sign,

we build stupas by the replicas of Buddha,

happiness is in the air,

we make prayer-flags for peace and for all.'

KARMA

Think good thoughts,

speak adorable words,

do good to others,

everything comes back.

Is it the essence of Karma?

I was wondering for the

unerring significance of Karma,

while sitting at that silent monastery.

I recalled what the Bhagawat Gita says,

'Everyone has to carry out swardharma

without carelessness and ego.'

So does Buddhism,

the eternal existence of the

chain of cause and effect!

FOUR NOBLE TRUTHS

Buddha's message,

we could grasp at that

serene place,

where peace is preached silently –

"There is suffering."

"There is a cause for suffering."

"There is an end of suffering."

"There is a path of practice that puts an end to suffering."

THE MONKS OF UGYENLING

Pursuing the noble eight-fold path,

right view, right aim, right speech,

right action, right livelihood,

right effort, right mindfulness

and right meditation,

the monks, in the Ugyenling monastery

sitting with their wise postures,

to pray silently.

We were blessed!

A STOREHOUSE OF WISDOM

As we entered the huge campus,

Zhichenkhar

beside the sparkling Thimphuchu river

we were swayed,

by the light,

probably the inner light,

the light of wisdom.

The place,

where mind, body and soul

are made to be in harmony.

They also measure

beauty in people's mind

and instil Buddha's messages of

excellence in body, mind and speech.,

when one has faith in one's fellow beings.

A fountainhead

of happiness.

A philosophy developed

to warm up human souls

in equal measure!

IN SEARCH OF BHUTAN

We were then above the layers of cloud,

the sun was playing hide and seek.

We were in a fluffy layer..

of clouds,

in the dizzy heights of Himalayas

the abode of the great God of the earth..

being welcomed by the white clouds...

and snow on one side.

As we landed,

"Time here flies one hour ahead of India..

The outside temperature is 7 degree Celsius,"

the cabin crew announced with welcoming warmth.

Crossing the Paro Chu river, we got the taste of

the air of Bhutan...

the mountain tops surrounded by

the uncommonly uniformed houses of the locals.

A stop-over at the confluence of Paro Chu and Wang Chu

offered us time to pray for the unseen..

also to discover at that twilight hour,

the compassionate statue of Lord Buddha,
watching us from His lofty height.

LADY WITH A FRESH SMILE

The lady with pink cheeks and

fresh smiles,

welcomed us

to her dainty shop..

A crowd of

little Buddhas

pulled me in.

As I looked around,

the Lord was everywhere,

even in so many colourful replicas...

and endearing key rings..

I bought many..

The Buddha smiles

even on the currency notes.

Her smiles,

told us the village

far away and behind that majestic mountain range,

to which she belongs.

A PRAYER AT DOCHULA

As we started ascending for

our pilgrimage,

we came across

several women,

sitting with unsullied smiles

like the local vegetables.

We drove through

snowflakes with sunshine

a good and rare sight

for those propitious.

Dochula,

a sacred place...

where heroes and patriots,

lie in eternal sleep

in silence and peace.

We offered our prayers for them,

without asking their names.

REBECCA

Determined

to preserve

the white-bellied heron,

a critically endangered bird

almost on the brink

of extinction,

Rebecca travels alone

along the banks of Punatshangchu.

A solitary species

seen alone or in pairs,

like her works

silent and unyielding.

'My grandfather was a naturalist,

so was my father,'

with pride, she said.

At The Tawang Monastery

"To love the bird,

you love the fish,

and to love the fish,

you love the river,'
Rebecca told me,
worried, as marshlands disappear,
one by one,
rapidly.
With her determination,
to save the bird,
gifted me a book,
precious to preserve,
like the bird.

A POEM FOR THIMPHU

Visiting this new country, new place,

new folds of the mountain,

where wind and silence

sing duets for me.

Sitting on the lap of the soaring mountain

I hear another song,

as snow crowns every peak with dazzling white.

Spending two days at Taj Tashi, Thimphu,

the feeling of heavenly presence

overpowers me.

I prayed to the Lord

spinning the prayer wheels

seven times in a row,

chanting silently

Om mani padma hum

Om mani padma hum.

NATIONAL MEMORIAL CHORTEN

After offering our prayers at

the monastery,

in the heart of Thimphu,

we came out with

a peaceful mind.

I looked around,

near the wheels of Karma,

where elderly people

were chatting

in a relaxed way in that morning hour,

as the sun kept showering its

sun-shine sparingly.

Yet, for them a paradise

for talking with the souls.

AT THE GUEST HOUSE

Only silence speaks here,
nothing else.
The silent mountain about to close
its day's activities.

The sun was about to leave and bid adieu,
for another day.
While sitting at that cosy suit,
gradually the sun disappeared in
the folds of the Himalayas,
and darkness enveloped
everything...
I prayed to express my
gratitude to witness
that divine moment...

AT THE TAWANG MONASTERY

It was around 4 o'clock in the evening.

We were at the main entrance of the monastery.

The little boy-lamas were playing in the stone courtyard of the
Monastery.

We were awestruck to see the kids in Lama's dress.

Why do their parents offer such little ones to follow,

a hard path to salvation?

Roaming around the place,

we felt,

are they poor?

Certainly not.

All richness of wisdom

in their mind and spirit.

This is the land

which has been supporting the

monastery

to stand boldly with determination and honesty.

The cold wind blowing from the eastern Himalayas

purified our soul to the utmost core.

And we realised…

'we are so little creatures,

beside the huge stretched mountain...'

.....

On entering the monastery,

we discovered the upper sides of the inner walls

painted brightly

with murals

of divinities and saints,

the monks sitting for their evening prayers.

We came out,

the monastery stood

with loving eyes

to bless the

Tawangchu valley below.

The cold wind blowing from

the distant ridges of the Himalayas

came forward to welcome us...

We sat down at the rock stairs..

to take rest.

Prevailing peace engulfed us and everywhere....

as the little lamas greeted us so tenderly.

Was that the entry point to the doors to Heaven?

We were blessed...

for being capable of riding up

only with our determination...
The division and dissimilarity
regardless of religions seemed to
disappear at the gate
of the Tawang Monastery.
We were bound to feel soothingly.

THE MUSEUM

Stepping into the showroom,

outside the war memorial,

to pick up a few mementoes,

I landed up amidst

a hundred Buddhas,

smiling, sleeping,

meditating,

a few raising their hands,

of clay, wood,

and metal too,

and also in paintings,

drawn by nameless monks,

big and small.

We would certainly preserve them

as charming memories

to our visit

to Tawang..

And as I turned back,

a poster caught my attention,

"We lost the war

because we did not

have equipments,

now we are prepared."

REMEMBERING RUPA

The lady with a beautiful smile

greeted us from the core of

her sparkling heart like the swift flowing river nearby.

We stood at the confluence of

Ziging kho and Dunik kho rivers,

with an intention

to meet Rupa.

Grasping

the tune of her true love,

though met for the first time,

we felt as if we knew

each other from a long time...

A time, when a Tibetan prince married Rupa,

an Assamese prince,

and then,

Japtang, their son, became the king,

of Rupa,

of the Sherdukpans.

Did the lady recognise us?

Did the lady remember Rupa?

ANI GOMPA

Unable to visit
the Ani Gompa,
but..
we heard more about the nunnery,
where fifty ascetic women reside,
though we could not make it.
Like the Monpa boys,
the Monpa girls also
lead a life of
Buddhist Bhikshuni.
Loitering around the monastery,
we could realise passionately,
from the faces of the little lamas,
about their aunts and sisters,
and the right path,
they have been treading
over the years.

STANDING AT BUMLA

I was vigorously aware of my surrounding,
beautiful snow-capped mountains around.
Silent cold engulfed us sharply.
We were closer to the top of the Himalayas,
we stood on McMahon Line!
We were at the Hall of Friendship..!
At the Heap of Stones, at the Rock of Peace!
We set foot on the soil of Tibet..
The aura had reminded me of
another visit,
when we could touch and feel
the soil beyond
from Nathula in Sikkim,
now, climbing up beyond Tawang.
A heavenly height!
I began to think
perhaps, the same route to Lord Shiva's abode
the Mount Kailash.....
Reaching the height

was like knocking at the door of Heaven!

Should we also knock

at our heart's door?

A blessing of knowledge,

we gathered at that intensely cold moment

like an awakening

from the deep slumber of ignorance…

we were indeed wakeful,

at that biting cold sipping hot tea,

the soldiers offered us,

and they told us to walk slowly.

I noticed from the corner of my eyes..

"Some people say love is important for life,

but I say oxygen is more important for life."

What next?

With folded hands,

we prayed at the top

with resolutions inside!